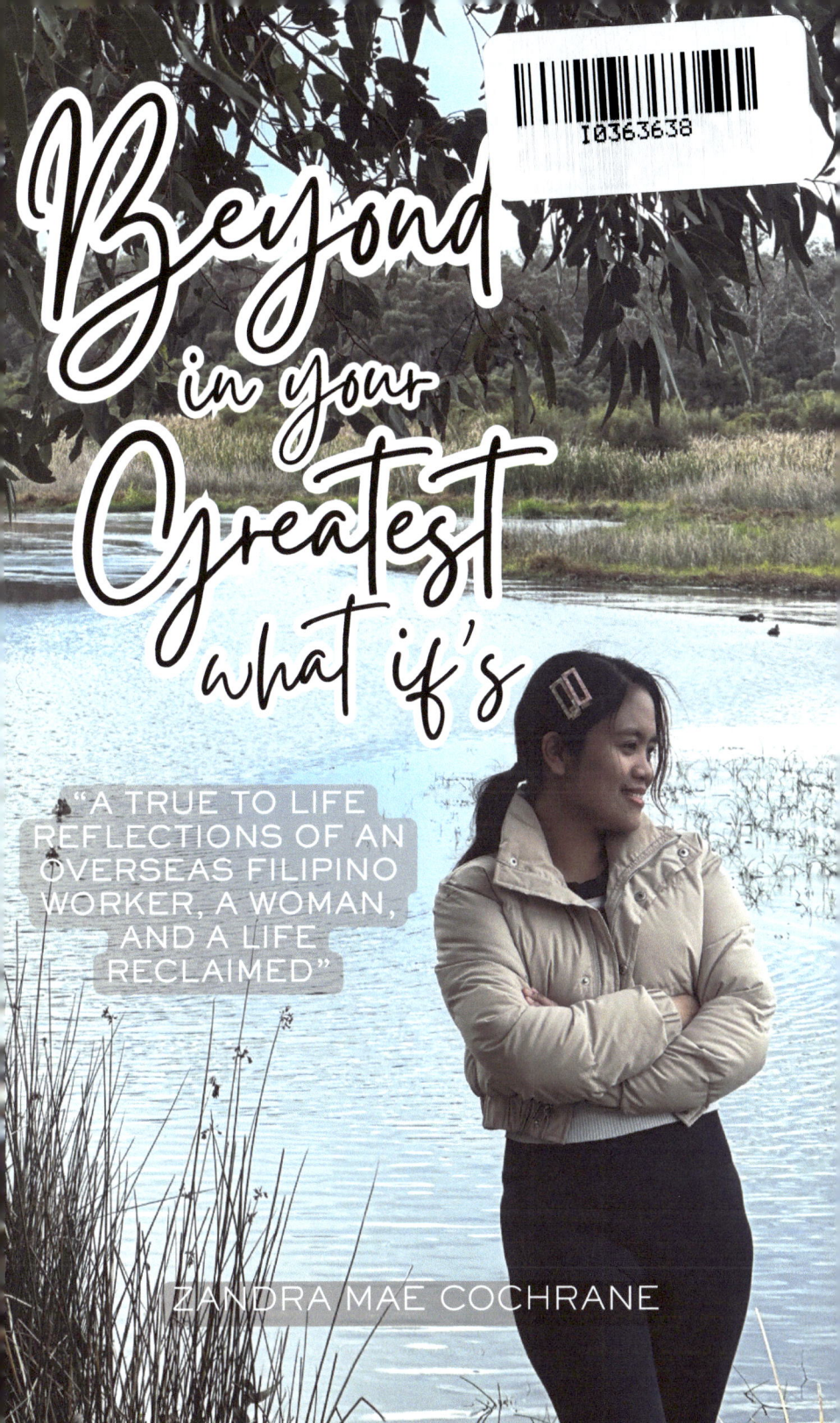

BEYOND IN YOUR GREATEST WHAT IF'S

"A TRUE TO LIFE REFLECTIONS OF AN OFW, A WOMAN, AND A LIFE RECLAIMED"

BY ZANDRA MAE COCHRANE

PERTH, WESTERN AUSTRALIA
2025

COPYRIGHT © 2025 BY ZANDRA MAE COCHRANE
ISBN: 978-1-7644630-1-0

ALL RIGHTS RESERVED.

NO PART OF THIS BOOK MAY BE REPRODUCED, STORED IN A RETRIEVAL SYSTEM, OR TRANSMITTED IN ANY FORM OR BY ANY MEANS—ELECTRONIC, MECHANICAL, PHOTOCOPYING, RECORDING, OR OTHERWISE—WITHOUT THE PRIOR WRITTEN PERMISSION OF THE AUTHOR.

THIS IS A WORK OF CREATIVE NONFICTION. NAMES, PLACES, AND EVENTS MAY HAVE BEEN CHANGED OR ADAPTED TO PROTECT PRIVACY AND ENHANCE NARRATIVE FLOW. ANY RESEMBLANCE TO ACTUAL PERSONS, LIVING OR DEAD, IS PURELY COINCIDENTAL UNLESS STATED OTHERWISE.

FOR INQUIRIES, PERMISSIONS, OR FEEDBACK,
CONTACT: ZANDRAMAECOCHRANE@GMAIL.COM

To the person I become

HAVE YOU EVER ASKED YOURSELF **"WHAT'S LIFE ALL ABOUT?"** I WONDER IF OTHER PEOPLE ALSO THINK THE SAME, LIFE IS FILLED WITH CROSSROADS—MOMENTS WHEN WE STOP AND WONDER, **"WHAT IF THINGS HAD GONE DIFFERENTLY?"**

SOMETIMES, I PAUSED AND ASKED MYSELF, "WHAT IF I HAD STAYED IN THE PHILIPPINES INSTEAD OF PURSUING AN UNCERTAIN FUTURE IN AUSTRALIA? WHAT IF I HAD CHOSEN TO REMAIN WITH MY CHILDREN, DEVOTING MYSELF ENTIRELY TO MOTHERHOOD? WHAT IF I HAD NEVER MET SIGNIFICANT PEOPLE HERE, NEVER TAKEN RISKS, NEVER FOUGHT THROUGH STRUGGLES THAT SEEMED IMPOSSIBLE TO OVERCOME?

FOR YEARS, THESE WHAT IFS ECHOED IN MY MIND, IT CERTAINLY SHAPED THE WAY I VIEWED MY JOURNEY. AS A PARENT, A DAUGHTER, AN OVERSEAS FILIPINO WORKER, AN EDUCATOR, AND A WOMAN WHO HAS SAILED THROUGH HARDSHIP WITH RESILIENCE, MY LIFE HAS BEEN SHAPED BY DECISIONS THAT COULD HAVE LED ME MAYBE IN MANY DIFFERENT DIRECTIONS.

ONE OF THE GREATEST STRUGGLES WAS CHOOSING TO LEAVE MY CHILDREN BEHIND, NOT BECAUSE I WANTED TO, BUT BECAUSE I BELIEVED THERE IS SOMETHING GREATER FOR THEIR FUTURE.

EVERY PART OF MY SOUL WANTED TO STAY, TO BE PRESENT FOR EVERY MILESTONE, & TO HOLD THEM CLOSE. BUT WHAT IF STAYING MEANT SACRIFICING THE OPPORTUNITIES THAT WOULD ONE DAY BUILD THE LIFE I DREAMED FOR THEM?

WHAT IF I HAD NEVER LEFT MY LIFE BEFORE? WOULD MY LIFE HAVE FELT MORE FAMILIAR, MORE SECURE? OR WOULD I HAVE STAYED WHERE I WAS, AND NEVER DISCOVERING WHAT I COULD BECOME?

THESE QUESTIONS ARE NOT JUST REFLECTIONS OF THE PAST. AT SOME POINT, THESE ARE REMINDERS OF THE CHOICES THAT SHAPE US— THE MOMENTS OF DOUBT, COURAGE, SACRIFICE, AND TRANSFORMATION.

THIS BOOK IS AN INVITATION TO REFLECT—NOT ONLY ON MY STORY BUT ON YOURS. IT IS ABOUT THE DECISIONS THAT DEFINE US, THE FEARS THAT CHALLENGE US, AND THE COURAGE IT TAKES TO MOVE FORWARD, EVEN WHEN UNCERTAINTY WHISPERS THAT WE SHOULD NOT.

SO I ASK YOU: WHAT IS YOUR GREATEST "WHAT IF?" AND MORE IMPORTANTLY—WILL YOU KEEP WALKING FORWARD TO SEE WHAT'S BEYOND IT?

WHAT IF I HAD STAYED IN THE PHILIPPINES?

I REMEMBER, THERE WAS A TIME WHEN I THOUGHT I WOULD NEVER LEAVE. THE PHILIPPINES WAS HOME FOR ME AND TO MANY FILIPINOS OUT THERE WORKING ABROAD, —IT IS THE PLACE WHERE MY ROOTS RAN DEEP, WHERE FAMILY, FAMILIARITY, CULTURE AND TRADITION HELD ME CLOSE.

LIFE WAS CHALLENGING BUT TO ME SOMETIMES, ITS PREDICTABLE. I KNEW THE STREETS, THE LANGUAGE, THE RHYTHM & ROUTINE OF DAILY LIFE. I HAD MY MOTHER, MY FATHER, MY BROTHER, MY CHILDREN, BUSINESS, WORK AND THE QUIET CERTAINTY THAT, NO MATTER HOW DIFFICULT THINGS BECAME, I COULD MAKE IT WORK.

BUT THEN, THE WHAT IF CREPT IN.

WHAT IF THERE WAS MORE BEYOND WHAT I ALREADY KNEW? WHAT IF LEAVING OPENED DOORS I HAD NEVER IMAGINED? WHAT IF STAYING MEANT LIMITING MYSELF TO THE COMFORTS OF THE KNOWN BUT NEVER DISCOVERING WHAT I COULD TRULY BECOME?

THE CHOICE TO LEAVE WASN'T SIMPLE AND EASY. IT WAS LAYERED WITH FEAR—FEAR OF FAILURE, FEAR OF LONELINESS, FEAR THAT I WOULD REGRET STEPPING AWAY FROM EVERYTHING I HAD BUILT. I THOUGHT ABOUT MY CHILDREN, ABOUT THE LIFE I WANTED TO GIVE THEM.

WOULD LEAVING THEM FOR AN OPPORTUNITY ELSEWHERE MEAN I HAD ABANDONED THEM? OR WOULD IT MEAN I HAD FOUGHT FOR THEM IN THE ONLY WAY I KNEW HOW—BY SECURING A FUTURE THAT OFFERED HOPE BEYOND SURVIVAL?

I REMEMBER STANDING OUTSIDE THE HOUSE, WAITING FOR THE BUS GOING TO AIRPORT, MY HEART WAS POUNDING, HANDS GRIPPING MY LUGGAGE AS THOUGH THEY WERE THE ONLY THINGS TETHERING ME TO COME BACK INSIDE THE HOME. MY MOTHER'S EYES HELD PRIDE AND WORRY IN EQUAL MEASURE. MY CHILDREN, TOO YOUNG TO UNDERSTAND, CLUNG TO ME. THOUGH HANIE, MY ELDEST LEARN A LITTLE BIT OF REASONS.

I WANTED TO STAY—I ALMOST DID. BUT SOMETHING IN ME WHISPERED, GO. TAKE THIS STEP. SEE WHAT IS BEYOND.

THEN HERE I CAME. AUSTRALIA WAS UNFAMILIAR, UNFORGIVING AT TIMES, AND RELENTLESSLY DEMANDING. THE CULTURE WAS DIFFERENT, THE EXPECTATIONS WERE HIGHER, AND THE MOMENTS OF LONELINESS CAME IN WAVES LIKE VAST WAVES IN THE OCEANS. BUT AS THE DAYS, MONTHS, AND YEARS PASSED, I FOUND MYSELF GROWING— AS AN OVERSEAS WORKER, AS A MOTHER, AND AS A PERSON TRYING TO SEE AN ENTIRELY NEW VERSION OF MYSELF.

IF I HAD STAYED IN THE PHILIPPINES, I WOULD HAVE BUILT A LIFE, NO DOUBT ON THAT. BUT IT WOULD HAVE BEEN A LIFE SHAPED BY PREDICTABILITY RATHER THAN POSSIBILITY. BY LEAVING, I DISCOVERED HOPE, FAITH & STRENGTH I NEVER KNEW I HAD. I LEARNED THAT HOME IS NOT JUST A PLACE—IT IS THE PEOPLE WHO HOLD YOU CLOSE, WHETHER NEAR OR FAR.

I STILL WONDER SOMETIMES—WHAT IF I HAD NEVER LEFT? WOULD MY CHILDREN HAVE KNOWN A DIFFERENT VERSION OF ME? WOULD I HAVE FOUND HAPPINESS IN THE FAMILIARITY? OR WOULD I HAVE SPENT MY YEARS WONDERING WHAT COULD HAVE BEEN?

PERHAPS I WOULD LIKE TO REMIND YOU THAT ONE OF THE GREATEST LESSON IS THIS — THERE IS NO RIGHT OR WRONG CHOICE, IT IS YOU WHO WILL DECIDE AND GET READY TO WHATEVER OUTCOME IT WILL LEAD US.

FOR ME, STEPPING INTO THE UNKNOWN WAS THE ONLY WAY TO SEE WHAT LIES BEYOND MY GREATEST WHAT IF.

I WANTED TO ASK YOU, WHAT PART OF YOUR PAST STILL CALLS TO YOU? IS IT A PLACE, A PERSON, OR A VERSION OF YOURSELF? WHAT HAVE YOU LEARNED FROM LEAVING — AND WHAT HAVE YOU GAINED BY CHOOSING A NEW PATH?

WHAT IF I HAD TAKEN A DIFFERENT CAREER PATH?

THERE WAS A TIME WHEN I WONDERED IF I WAS MEANT TO WALK A DIFFERENT ROAD.

EDUCATION WASN'T ALWAYS THE OBVIOUS CHOICE. I'VE BEEN INTO NURSING, BUSINESS, I COULD HAVE PURSUED SOMETHING ELSE—PERHAPS A CAREER OUTSIDE THE CLASSROOM, A PROFESSION THAT DIDN'T REQUIRE ME TO EXPERIENCE THE CHALLENGES OF BEING A TEACHER OR IMMERSE MYSELF IN BEHAVIORAL MANAGEMENT AND INDIVIDUALIZED LEARNING STRATEGIES.

THERE WERE DAYS I QUESTIONED WHETHER I HAD MADE THE RIGHT DECISION. DAYS WHEN EXHAUSTION SETTLED SO DEEP, WHEN CHALLENGES AT WORK FELT OVERWHELMING, WHEN I WONDERED IF MY EFFORTS WERE ENOUGH. AND THEN, **THE WHAT IF WOULD WHISPER—WHAT IF I HAD CHOSEN A DIFFERENT PATH?**

WHAT IF I HAD VENTURED INTO A CAREER THAT DIDN'T DEMAND SO MUCH EMOTIONAL INVESTMENT? ONE THAT DIDN'T PLACE ME IN THE HEART OF STUDENTS' STRUGGLES, SHAPING THEIR FUTURES IN WAYS THAT SOME-

FELT UNSEEN? WHAT IF I HAD PURSUED SOMETHING ELSE LIKE OFFICE, HOSPITAL CARES OR TECHNOLOGICAL INDUSTRIES, WORKING AS FULL-TIME INSTEAD OF EDUCATION? FOR A LONG TIME, THE ANSWERS WERE UNCLEAR. BUT THEN, MOMENTS HAPPENED— SMALL VICTORIES, BREAKTHROUGHS WITH STUDENTS, THE JOY OF WITNESSING A CHILD EXPRESS THEMSELVES FOR THE FIRST TIME THROUGH DIFFERENT TOOLS OR PLAY.

I REALIZED THEN THAT TEACHING WASN'T JUST A PROFESSION—IT WAS A CALLING. IF YOU THINK ABOUT PROFESSION, IT WASN'T JUST ABOUT CHOOSING THE EASIEST PATH, BUT THE ONE WHERE I COULD MAKE A DIFFERENCE.

HAD I CHOSEN ANOTHER CAREER, MAYBE LIFE WOULD HAVE BEEN DIFFERENT. BUT WOULD IT HAVE BEEN MORE FULFILLING? WOULD IT HAVE GIVEN ME THE SAME SENSE OF PURPOSE, THE KNOWLEDGE THAT EACH DAY I SHOW UP, I'M SHAPING SOMEONE'S FUTURE?

IN THIS WHAT IF'S OF MINE, ONE LESSON I REALIZED THAT SOMETIMES, THE HARDEST CHOICES CAN LEAD US TO THE BEST DESTINATIONS. SOMETIMES IT'S HARD TO EMBRACE CHANGES BUT AS FOR ME, STAYING IN MY PRESENT CAREER NOW, MEANT EMBRACING SOMETHING FAR GREATER THAN MYSELF.

WHAT IF I HAD GIVEN UP MY LIFE?

I REMEMBERED, THERE WERE MOMENTS WHEN I WONDERED IF CONTINUING WAS EVEN WORTH IT.

JUGGLING MULTIPLE JOBS, TRYING TO MAKE ENDS MEET, CARRYING THE WEIGHT OF FINANCIAL BURDENS—ALL WHILE BEING A MOTHER, AN EMPLOYEE, AND A WOMAN FACING LIFE'S RELENTLESS CHALLENGES. THERE WERE NIGHTS WHEN EXHAUSTION FELT HEAVIER THAN HOPE, WHEN THE STRUGGLE TO SURVIVE SEEMED GREATER THAN THE DESIRE TO DREAM.

WHAT IF I HAD CHOSEN TO STOP? TO WALK AWAY FROM EVERYTHING I HAD BUILT, TO LET GO OF THE AMBITIONS I FOUGHT SO HARD TO HOLD ONTO? WHAT IF I HAD SIMPLY SURRENDERED TO THE WEIGHT OF IT ALL?

THE TRUTH IS, I THOUGHT ABOUT IT. MANY TIMES.

I IMAGINED A LIFE WHERE I NO LONGER HAD TO WORRY ABOUT DEBT, SURVIVAL, OR EXPECTATIONS.

A LIFE WHERE I DIDN'T HAVE TO BALANCE BETWEEN RESPONSIBILITIES THAT OFTEN FELT IMPOSSIBLE TO MANAGE. BUT EVERY TIME I STOOD ON THE EDGE OF GIVING UP, SOMETHING PULLED ME BACK—A REMINDER OF WHY I STARTED, WHO I WAS FIGHTING FOR, AND THE FUTURE I REFUSED TO LOSE SIGHT OF.

THEN I THOUGHT HOW GREAT IS OUR GOD THAT HE ALLOWS ME TO KEPT GOING.

BECAUSE EVEN ON THE HARDEST DAYS, I KNEW THAT STOPPING WOULDN'T BRING RELIEF—IT WOULD ONLY BRING REGRET. BECAUSE EVERY SACRIFICE I MADE WAS FOR SOMETHING GREATER THAN MYSELF—FOR MY CHILDREN, FOR MY FAMILY, FOR THE LIFE I WANTED TO CREATE BEYOND STRUGGLE AND ABOVE, FOR THE GLORY TO GOD.

HAD I GIVEN UP, I WOULDN'T HAVE SEEN THE MOMENTS OF VICTORY—THE SMALL WINS, THE BREAKTHROUGHS, THE PROOF THAT MY EFFORTS MATTERED. I WOULDN'T HAVE BEEN ABLE TO LOOK BACK AND SAY, I SURVIVED THAT. I MADE IT THROUGH. SOMETIMES, WE KEPT LEANING IN THE PAST FAILURES AND PAINS IN OUR LIVES WITHOUT SEEING OUR SMALL WINS.

WELL, THE GREATEST LESSON IN THIS WHAT IF IS THIS: STRENGTH ISN'T ABOUT NEVER

—IT'S ABOUT CHOOSING TO KEEP GOING EVEN WHEN EVERYTHING TELLS YOU TO STOP.

AND FOR ME, CHOOSING TO KEEP GOING MEANT REFUSING TO LET MY CIRCUMSTANCES DEFINE MY FUTURE.

WHEN DID YOU FEEL LIKE GIVING UP — AND WHAT KEPT YOU GOING? WHO OR WHAT REMINDED YOU OF YOUR WORTH? I HOPE YOU LET THAT MEMORY BE YOUR ANCHOR.

WHAT IF I HAD NO MORE TIME TO BE WITH MY LOVED ONES?

A PRIEST ONCE TOLD DURING ITS HOMILY IN THE CHURCH, "DO YOU WANT TO DIE NOW?", A LOT OF US SAID "NOT YET FATHER", THEN HE RESPONDED, " I GUESS, YOU ALL NEVER KNOW HOW MANY TIMES WE DIED, AND YOU KNOW WHAT IS IT? THAT IS HEARTACHES". I PAUSED AND THINK. THEN I THOUGHT ABOUT GRIEF. FELT LIKE I DIE. IT HAS A WAY OF RESHAPING OUR MEMORIES, MAKING US LINGER ON THE MOMENTS WE NEVER HAD ENOUGH OF.

I OFTEN WONDER—WHAT IF I HAD MORE TIME WITH MY FATHER? WOULD I HAVE LEARNED MORE FROM HIM, UNDERSTOOD HIS WISDOM DIFFERENTLY, FELT HIS PRESENCE IN THE MOMENTS WHEN I NEEDED IT THE MOST? THAT'S HOW I ACKNOWLEDGE THAT KIND OF WHAT IF, WHEN I STARTED LIVING MYSELF ALONE AND AWAY IN MY COMFORT ZONE.

I HAVE LEARNED THAT LOSING HIM WAS NOT JUST THE LOSS OF A PARENT—IT WAS THE LOSS OF SECURITY, GUIDANCE, AND THE QUIET ASSURANCE THAT SOMEONE WAS ALWAYS THERE TO PROTECT ME.

OVERNIGHT, I STEPPED INTO THE ROLE OF THE ELDEST, CARRYING THE WEIGHT OF RESPONSIBILITY, OF BEING STRONG FOR EVERYONE ELSE EVEN WHEN I FELT I DON'T KNOW HOW. IT SEEMS LIKE I HAVE NO CHOICE, BUT THE ONLY CHOICE IS TO BE STRONG.

HAD I HAD MORE TIME, MAYBE I WOULD HAVE ASKED HIM MORE QUESTIONS ABOUT PARENTHOOD. MAYBE I WOULD HAVE TOLD HIM ABOUT MY DREAMS HERE IN AUSTRALIA, MY FEARS, THE THINGS I NEVER SAID OUT LOUD. MAYBE I WOULD HAVE SHARED MORE LAUGHTER ESPECIALLY EATING OUTSIDE THE HOUSE WITH OUR FAVORITE FILIPINO PORK LECHON, MAYBE I COULD HAVE HELD ONTO HIS VOICE A LITTLE LONGER, MEMORIZED EVERY MOMENT INSTEAD OF ASSUMING TIME WAS ALWAYS ON OUR SIDE.

BUT TIME WASN'T. AND GRIEF DOESN'T COME WITH SECOND CHANCES.

I'VE LEARNED THAT LOSS NEVER REALLY LEAVES US—IT BECOMES PART OF WHO WE ARE. IT SHAPES THE WAY WE LOVE, THE WAY WE FIGHT FOR OUR FUTURES, THE WAY WE CHERISH THE PEOPLE STILL WITH US.

MAYBE I NEVER HAD ENOUGH TIME WITH HIM. BUT IN THE LESSONS HE LEFT SO MANY THINGS BEHIND, ESPECIALLY IN THE STRENGTH I CARRY BECAUSE OF HIM, MAYBE I HAVE JUST ENOUGH TO KEEP MOVING FORWARD.

WHAT IF I NEVER MET MY OTHER HALF?

THERE ARE MOMENTS IN LIFE WHEN ONE UNEXPECTED MEETING CHANGES EVERYTHING. I GUESS YOU ALREADY HAD A GLIMPSE OF AN IDEA WHAT IM REFERRING FOR, THE OTHER HALF OF OUR LIFE.

WHAT IF I HAD NEVER MET MY OTHER HALF? WOULD AUSTRALIA HAVE FELT DIFFERENT—LESS LIKE HOME, MORE LIKE JUST ANOTHER PLACE ON A MAP? WOULD MY LIFE HAVE FELT EMPTIER, MISSING THE WARMTH OF HAVING SOMEONE WHO TRULY SEES ME AND CHOOSES TO STAND BY MY SIDE?

HONESTLY WHEN WE MET, I WASN'T SEARCHING FOR LOVE, YET HE BECAME THE QUIET PRESENCE THAT MADE EVERY CHALLENGE FEEL LIGHTER, EVERY DAY MORE MEANINGFUL. THAT PERSON TAUGHT ME THAT LOVE ISN'T JUST ABOUT EMOTIONS— IT'S ABOUT CHOOSING A PERSON, ACCEPTING THEM FULLY, AND EMBRACING THE LIFE YOU BUILD TOGETHER. IT WAS NOT A DRAMATIC, WHIRLWIND ROMANCE. THERE WERE NO MOVIE-LIKE MOMENTS WHERE EVERYTHING SUDDENLY FELL INTO PLACE. BUT SLOWLY, STEADILY, HE BECAME THE QUIET PRESENCE THAT MADE LIFE HERE MORE MEANINGFUL, MORE PEACEFUL, MORE COMPLETE.

CHOOSING TO STAY WITH MY OTHER HALF WAS NEVER A QUESTION—IT WAS THE EASIEST DECISION AND IN COUNTLESS WAYS I EVER MADE. CHOOSING HIS PEACE, HIS KINDNESS, HIS COMPANIONSHIP BECAME A FOUNDATION THAT MADE LIFE IN AUSTRALIA FEEL WHOLE.

HAD I NEVER MET HIM, MAYBE I WOULD HAVE FACE THIS JOURNEY ALONE. BUT BECAUSE I DID, I GET TO WALK FORWARD WITH SOMEONE WHO UNDERSTANDS ME, SUPPORTS ME, AND SHARES THIS LIFE WITH ME—THROUGH EVERY STRUGGLE, EVERY DREAM, AND EVERY ORDINARY MOMENT IN BETWEEN.

THERE ARE MANY PEOPLE WE MEET IN OUR LIFETIME—SOME STAY, SOME LEAVE, AND SOME CHANGE US COMPLETELY. MEETING OUR OTHER HALF WASN'T JUST A MOMENT; IT WAS A TURNING POINT. IT WAS FINDING HOME IN A PERSON, NOT JUST A PLACE.

THERE WILL BE PEOPLE THAT WILL WALK INTO OUR LIFE BY CHANCE. OTHERS STAY BECAUSE THEY ARE MEANT TO. AND WITH MY OTHER HALF, I KNEW FROM THE BEGINNING—I WASN'T JUST MEETING SOMEONE, I WAS CHOOSING MY PERSON. AND IN CHOOSING, I FOUND SOMETHING FAR MORE LASTING THAN LOVE ALONE— I FOUND A PARTNER, A SAFE SPACE, AND THE FUTURE I NEVER EXPECTED BUT NOW CAN'T IMAGINE LIVING WITHOUT.

WHAT IF I NEVER LEARNED THE POWER OF SAYING NO?

THERE WAS A TIME WHEN I BELIEVED THAT SAYING "NO" MEANT I WAS BEING DISRESPECTFUL AND DIFFICULT. CULTURALLY AND TRADITIONALLY, I WAS RAISED TO BE RESPECTFUL, ACCOMMODATING, HOSPITABLE AND GRATEFUL TO WHATEVER WE HAD IN OUR HANDS WHETHER SMALL OR BIG— MOST ESPECIALLY IN SYSTEMS WHERE I FELT LIKE A GUEST OR A VISITOR. AS AN OFW, AND A MOTHER TRYING TO LEARN UNFAMILIAR THINGS, I OFTEN FELT THE PRESSURE TO COMPLY, EVEN WHEN SOMETHING DIDN'T FEEL RIGHT. I ALWAYS FELT OF BEING OBLIGATED.

AND YOU KNOW WHAT? I SAID YES TO LONG WAITS, CONFUSING INSTRUCTIONS, AND MOST OF THE TIME, THE EMOTIONAL DISCOMFORT, BECAUSE I THOUGHT THAT WAS THE PRICE OF BEING ACCEPTED. BUT DEEP DOWN, EVERY "YES" THAT BETRAYED MY BOUNDARIES LEFT A QUIET BRUISE ON MY SPIRIT AND SOUL.

ONE THING I HAVE SEEN, FOR MANY FILIPINO OVERSEAS WORKERS, SAYING "NO" TO FAMILY BACK HOME FEELS LIKE BETRAYAL BECAUSE WE WERE RAISED TO GIVE, TO SACRIFICE, TO CARRY THE WEIGHT OF OTHERS WITHOUT COMPLAINT. BUT THEY DON'T REALIZED THAT BEHIND EVERY

REMITTANCE IS A STORY – OF SKIPPED MEALS, KILOMETERS WALK, SILENT EXHAUSTION, AND DREAMS DEFERRED. I'VE LEARNED THAT LOVE DOESN'T MEAN ENDLESS GIVING. IT MEANS KNOWING WHEN TO PAUSE, WHEN TO PROTECT YOUR OWN STABILITY, AND WHEN TO SAY, "I WISH I COULD, BUT I CAN'T RIGHT NOW."

SAYING NO DOESN'T MEAN I LOVE THEM LESS. IT MEANS I'M CHOOSING TO BUILD A LIFE THAT ISN'T CONSTANTLY ON THE EDGE OF COLLAPSE. IT MEANS I'M HONORING THE HARD WORK I'VE DONE ABROAD – NOT JUST FOR THEM, BUT FOR MYSELF TOO.

ANOTHER ONE TURNING POINT CAME, WHEN I WAS SCHEDULED TO GET AN NBI IN THE PHILIPPINE CONSULATE OFFICE FOR FINGERPRINTING. TO BE HONEST, I HAD A TERRIBLE EXPERIENCED WHICH BROUGHT ME EMOTIONAL DISTRESS THERE – THE KIND THAT LINGERS LONG AFTER YOU LEAVE THE BUILDING. I KNEW I COULD FOLLOW THE INSTRUCTION, KEEP THE PEACE, AND AVOID QUESTIONS. BUT I ALSO KNEW THAT DOING SO WOULD MEAN IGNORING MY OWN EMOTIONAL SAFETY. THEY ASKED ME TO RETURN IN THE OFFICE AFTER THAT, BUT SO I SAID NO. NOT WITH ANGER, BUT WITH CLARITY. I FOUND AN ALTERNATIVE – THE BALLAJURA POLICE STATION – AND I MADE IT WORK.

THAT DECISION WASN'T JUST LOGISTICAL. IT WAS A DECLARATION: I DESERVE TO FEEL SAFE, EVEN IN OFFICIAL SPACES.

I GUESS SOME OF US DONT REALIZE THAT LEARNING TO SAY NO DIDN'T HAPPEN OVERNIGHT. THAT'S WHEN I LEARN THAT SAYING NO CAN COME IN QUIET MOMENTS – CHOOSING AND ASKING FOR HELP WHEN I FELT OVERWHELMED, AND REFUSING TO LET URGENCY OVERRIDE MY NEED FOR CONSISTENCY. EACH TIME I SAID NO, I FELT A FLICKER OF GUILT, FOLLOWED BY A WAVE OF RELIEF. I WASN'T BEING DEFIANT. I WAS BEING HONEST. AND IN THAT HONESTY, I FOUND A VERSION OF MYSELF THAT WAS NO LONGER AFRAID TO TAKE UP SPACE.

I'VE MET ALSO WOMEN WHO STAYED SILENT FOR YEARS, BELIEVING THAT LOVE MEANT ENDURANCE. ONE PARTNER, LING, USED TO APOLOGIZE EVERY TIME SHE ASKED FOR REST. HER HUSBAND EXPECTED DINNER AT 6:30, LAUNDRY FOLDED, AND HER SMILE READY – EVEN AFTER HER LONG SHIFT. ONE DAY, SHE CAME HOME, DROPPED THE GROCERY BAGS, AND SAID, "NO MORE." IT WASN'T LOUD. IT WASN'T DRAMATIC. BUT IT WAS THE BEGINNING OF HER FREEDOM. SHE STARTED TAKING WALKS ALONE,

EATING BEFORE COOKING, AND EVENTUALLY, ASKING FOR COUNSELING. HER "NO" DIDN'T BREAK HER MARRIAGE – IT SAVED HER. THEN THERE'S AMAR, WHO LEARNED TO SAY NO TO MANIPULATION DISGUISED AS ROMANCE. HER PARTNER WOULD GUILT HER INTO GIVING MONEY, ISOLATING HER FROM FRIENDS, AND CALLING IT LOVE. SHE FELT TRAPPED BETWEEN LOYALTY AND EXHAUSTION. THE DAY SHE SAID, "NO, I WON'T SEND MONEY THIS TIME," SHE CRIED – NOT BECAUSE SHE WAS CRUEL, BUT BECAUSE SHE WAS FINALLY KIND TO HERSELF. THAT "NO" LED TO BOUNDARIES, TO THERAPY, TO A VERSION OF HERSELF SHE HADN'T SEEN IN YEARS.

AND THERE'S THE QUIET REBELLION OF EVERYDAY FATIGUE. PARTNERS LIKE JOY, WHO CARRY THE INVISIBLE WEIGHT OF HOUSEHOLD CHORES, EMOTIONAL LABOR, AND CAREGIVING. SHE USED TO CLEAN IN SILENCE, COOK WITHOUT THANKS, AND COLLAPSE WITHOUT COMPLAINT. UNTIL ONE EVENING, SHE LOOKED AT THE PILE OF DISHES AND WHISPERED, "NOT TONIGHT." SHE SAT WITH TEA, WATCHED THE SUNSET, AND LET THE MESS WAIT. THAT "NO" WASN'T LAZINESS – IT WAS A RECLAIMING OF BREATH.

I'VE LEARNED THAT SAYING NO DOESN'T MEAN YOU LOVE LESS. IT MEANS YOU LOVE WISELY. IT MEANS YOU'VE STOPPED TRADING YOUR PEACE FOR SOMEONE ELSE'S COMFORT. IT MEANS YOU'RE CHOOSING TRUTH OVER PERFORMANCE.

WHAT IF SAYING NO IS THE BEGINNING OF HEALING? OF REWRITING THE RULES? OF TEACHING YOUR CHILDREN THAT LOVE INCLUDES REST, RESPECT, AND RECIPROCITY?

LET ME HELP YOU INTERNALIZE THESE PHRASE, "I SAY NO NOW – TO DISRESPECT, TO OVERWORK, TO EMOTIONAL GUILT. AND IN DOING SO, I SAY YES TO MYSELF. TO JOY. TO BOUNDARIES. TO THE KIND OF LOVE THAT DOESN'T ASK ME TO DISAPPEAR."

SAYING NO TAUGHT ME THAT BOUNDARIES ARE NOT WALLS – THEY ARE BRIDGES TO SELF-RESPECT. THEY ALLOW US TO PARTICIPATE IN SYSTEMS WITHOUT LOSING OURSELVES IN THEM. I'VE LEARNED THAT COMPLIANCE WITHOUT DIGNITY IS NOT PEACE – IT'S SILENCE. AND I REFUSE TO BE SILENT ABOUT WHAT I NEED, WHAT I FEEL, AND WHAT I DESERVE. MY NO IS NOT REJECTION. IT'S PROTECTION. IT'S THE VOICE OF A WOMAN WHO HAS LEARNED TO TRUST HER INSTINCTS, EVEN WHEN THE WORLD TELLS HER TO DOUBT THEM.

IF I HAD NEVER LEARNED THE POWER OF SAYING NO, I WOULD STILL BE SHRINKING TO FIT INTO SPACES THAT WERE NEVER MEANT FOR ME. I WOULD STILL BE APOLOGIZING FOR NEEDING CLARITY, REST, OR EMOTIONAL SAFETY. BUT I DID LEARN. AND NOW, EVERY BOUNDARY I SET IS A QUIET ACT OF LOVE — FOR MYSELF, FOR MY FUTURE, AND FOR THE LIFE I'M BUILDING WITH COURAGE AND CARE.

WHAT IF I HAD KNOWN THEN WHAT I KNOW NOW?

HAVE YOU TAUGHT ABOUT THIS QUESTION? WHAT IF I HAD KNOWN THEN WHAT I KNOW NOW? OF COURSE YOU WOULD ANSWER STRAIGHTAWAY,"IT WOULD BE BORING!". WOULD I HAVE LEFT WITH LESS FEAR, OR MORE GRACE? WOULD I HAVE HELD MYSELF WITH GENTLER HANDS, INSTEAD OF TRYING TO BE STRONG ALL THE TIME? I OFTEN THINK ABOUT THE GIRL I USED TO BE – PACKING HER BAGS WITH TREMBLING HOPE, SAYING GOODBYE WITH A BRAVE SMILE, AND STEPPING INTO A WORLD SHE DIDN'T YET UNDERSTAND. IF I COULD WRITE HER A LETTER, I WOULDN'T CHANGE HER PATH. I WOULD SIMPLY REMIND HER THAT SHE WAS NEVER ALONE, AND THAT EVERY TEAR, EVERY TRIUMPH, EVERY QUIET ACT OF COURAGE WAS WORTH IT.

I WILL SHARE TO YOU A LETTER THAT I HAVE WRITTEN FOR MY YOUNGER SELF.

DEAREST YOUNGER ME,

YOU WERE SO BRAVE, EVEN WHEN YOU DIDN'T FEEL IT. I STILL REMEMBER THE WAY YOU PACKED YOUR BAGS – NOT JUST WITH CLOTHES AND DOCUMENTS, BUT WITH QUIET HOPE AND

UNSPOKEN FEARS. YOU SMILED FOR EVERYONE ELSE, BUT INSIDE, YOU WERE TREMBLING. YOU DIDN'T KNOW WHAT WAS WAITING FOR YOU ON THE OTHER SIDE OF THAT PLANE RIDE, BUT YOU WENT ANYWAY. THAT WAS COURAGE, EVEN IF NO ONE CALLED IT THAT.

I WISH YOU HAD KNOWN THAT LEAVING HOME DIDN'T MEAN LEAVING BEHIND WHO YOU ARE. YOU CARRIED YOUR VALUES, YOUR FAITH, AND YOUR LOVE IN EVERY STEP. YOU WERE NEVER JUST AN OFW — YOU WERE A WOMAN AND A MOTHER WITH A STORY, A HEART, AND A PURPOSE. YOU DIDN'T HAVE TO PROVE YOUR WORTH TO ANYONE. YOU WERE ALREADY WORTHY, EVEN BEFORE THE VISA, THE DIPLOMA, OR THE JOB.

THERE WERE DAYS YOU FELT INVISIBLE. DAYS WHEN THE SYSTEM MADE YOU FEEL LIKE A NUMBER, NOT A PERSON. I WISH YOU HAD KNOWN THAT YOUR VOICE MATTERED. THAT YOU DIDN'T HAVE TO STAY SILENT JUST TO BE ACCEPTED. SAYING "NO" WASN'T DEFIANCE — IT WAS SELF-RESPECT. YOU DIDN'T OWE ANYONE YOUR PEACE. YOU OWED IT TO YOURSELF TO PROTECT IT.

YOU WORKED SO HARD, EVEN WHEN YOU WERE TIRED. YOU STUDIED LATE INTO THE NIGHT, SHOWED UP FOR WORK WITH A HEAVY HEART, AND KEPT GOING WHEN NO ONE WAS WATCHING. I WISH YOU HAD KNOWN THAT REST IS NOT WEAKNESS. THAT ASKING FOR HELP IS NOT FAILURE. YOU DIDN'T HAVE TO CARRY EVERYTHING ALONE. BUT YOU DID – AND I'M PROUD OF YOU FOR IT.

I REMEMBER THE MOMENTS YOU MISSED YOUR FAMILY. THE BIRTHDAYS, THE CHRISTMAS, NEW YEAR, HOLIDAYS, THE JOYFUL SIMPLE DINNERS YOU USED TO LOVE. I WISH YOU HAD KNOWN THAT LOVE STRETCHES ACROSS OCEANS. THAT EVEN IN YOUR ABSENCE, YOU WERE PRESENT IN THEIR HEARTS. YOU DIDN'T ABANDON THEM – YOU WERE BUILDING SOMETHING FOR THEM, AND FOR YOURSELF.

YOU GAVE EVEN WHEN YOU HAD LITTLE. YOU SENT MONEY HOME, ANSWERED EVERY REQUEST, AND FELT GUILTY WHEN YOU COULDN'T GIVE MORE. I WISH YOU HAD KNOWN THAT BOUNDARIES ARE NOT SELFISH. THAT SAYING "I CAN'T RIGHT NOW" IS NOT A BETRAYAL. YOU WERE ALLOWED TO KEEP SOMETHING FOR YOURSELF – YOUR ENERGY, YOUR SAVINGS, YOUR DREAMS.

YOU FELL IN LOVE, AND IT CHANGED YOU. YOU LEARNED TO TRUST AGAIN, TO BUILD A HOME IN A NEW LAND, TO BLEND CULTURES WITH GRACE. I WISH YOU HAD KNOWN THAT LOVE DOESN'T HAVE TO BE PERFECT TO BE REAL. THAT YOU DESERVED TENDERNESS, HONESTY, AND SOMEONE WHO SEES YOUR STRENGTH EVEN WHEN YOU FORGET IT.

IF I COULD HOLD YOUR HAND, I'D TELL YOU TO REST MORE. TO TRUST YOURSELF MORE. TO SAY NO WHEN SOMETHING DOESN'T FEEL RIGHT. YOU DON'T OWE ANYONE YOUR SILENCE. YOU OWE YOURSELF PEACE.

YOU FACED REJECTION, CONFUSION, AND FEAR. IMMIGRATION FORMS, CONSULATE AND OFFICE VISITS, — ALL OF IT TESTED YOUR PATIENCE AND YOUR SPIRIT. I WISH YOU HAD KNOWN THAT EVERY CHALLENGE WAS SHAPING YOU. THAT YOUR RESILIENCE WAS BEING CARVED IN SILENCE. YOU DIDN'T JUST SURVIVE — YOU TRANSFORMED.

YOU BUILT A LIFE. I WISH YOU HAD KNOWN HOW PROUD YOU WOULD BE ONE DAY — NOT JUST OF THE MILESTONES, BUT OF THE WOMAN YOU BECAME. YOU DIDN'T JUST CHASE A DREAM. YOU BECAME THE DREAM. YOU ARE LIVING PROOF THAT QUIET STRENGTH CAN MOVE MOUNTAINS.

SO THANK YOU. THANK YOU FOR BEING THE FOUNDATION OF EVERYTHING I AM NOW. I CARRY YOU WITH ME – IN EVERY DECISION, EVERY BOUNDARY, EVERY ACT OF LOVE. YOU WERE ENOUGH THEN. YOU ARE ENOUGH NOW. AND IF I COULD GO BACK, I WOULDN'T CHANGE YOUR PATH. I WOULD JUST HOLD YOUR HAND AND WHISPER, "YOU'RE DOING BETTER THAN YOU THINK."

WHAT IF I HAD NEVER KNOWN GOD?

THERE ARE QUESTIONS THAT HAUNT US QUIETLY, NOT WITH FEAR, BUT WITH AWE. THIS IS ONE OF MINE.

WHAT IF I HAD NEVER KNOWN JESUS? WHAT IF I HAD NEVER FELT THE WARMTH OF HIS GOODNESS, THE WHISPER OF HIS PRESENCE IN THE LONELIEST CORNERS OF MY LIFE?

I THINK ABOUT THE WOMAN I USED TO BE — STRONG, YES, BUT TIRED. ALWAYS CARRYING, ALWAYS GIVING, ALWAYS SURVIVING. I KNEW HOW TO ENDURE, HOW TO SMILE THROUGH STORMS, HOW TO KEEP MOVING EVEN WHEN MY HEART FELT LIKE IT WAS BREAKING IN SLOW MOTION. BUT I DIDN'T KNOW PEACE. NOT THE KIND THAT SITS WITH YOU IN SILENCE AND SAYS, YOU ARE NOT ALONE.

BEFORE I KNEW HIM, I THOUGHT STRENGTH MEANT NEVER ASKING FOR HELP. I THOUGHT HEALING MEANT FORGETTING. I THOUGHT LOVE HAD TO BE EARNED. BUT JESUS TAUGHT ME OTHERWISE.

HE MET ME IN THE QUIET. NOT IN GRAND MIRACLES OR THUNDEROUS SIGNS, BUT IN THE

SMALL MERCIES: A KIND WORD FROM A STRANGER, A MOMENT OF STILLNESS IN PRAYER, A DECISION THAT FELT TOO HEAVY UNTIL IT SUDDENLY DIDN'T. HE WAS THERE WHEN I LEFT THE PHILIPPINES, UNSURE OF WHO I'D BECOME. HE WAS THERE WHEN I STOOD IN FRONT OF IMMIGRATION OFFICERS, TREMBLING BUT DETERMINED. HE WAS THERE WHEN I CHOSE TO LOVE AGAIN – NOT BECAUSE I WAS WHOLE, BUT BECAUSE I WAS WILLING.

HIS GOODNESS DIDN'T ERASE MY PAIN. IT HELD IT. IT GAVE IT MEANING. IT TURNED MY "WHAT IFS" INTO "EVEN IFS."

EVEN IF I HAD FAILED. EVEN IF I HAD BEEN REJECTED. EVEN IF I HAD BEEN FORGOTTEN. HE WOULD STILL BE GOOD.

I THINK OF THE TIMES I COULD HAVE GIVEN UP – ON MYSELF, ON LOVE, ON HOPE. AND I WONDER: WOULD I HAVE SURVIVED WITHOUT HIM? MAYBE. BUT I WOULDN'T HAVE LIVED. NOT LIKE THIS. NOT WITH THIS QUIET JOY, THIS DEEP KNOWING, THIS GRACE THAT FLOWS THROUGH EVERY PAGE OF MY STORY.

SO YES, I ASK THE QUESTION. WHAT IF I HAD NEVER KNOWN JESUS? AND MY HEART ANSWERS: THEN I WOULD HAVE NEVER KNOWN MYSELF.

WHILE READING THIS, I WANTED TO ASK YOU, WHAT "WHAT IF" IN YOUR LIFE HAS LED YOU CLOSER TO GRACE? TAKE A MOMENT TO REFLECT. WAS IT A DECISION, A LOSS, A QUIET WHISPER? CAN YOU WRITE IT DOWN OR SPEAK IT ALOUD. I WANT TO REMIND YOU: YOU ARE NEVER ALONE.

"I WOULD HAVE LOST HEART, UNLESS I HAD BELIEVED THAT I WOULD SEE THE GOODNESS OF THE LORD IN THE LAND OF THE LIVING." — PSALM 27:13

LORD JESUS, THANK YOU FOR FINDING ME IN THE QUIET PLACES, FOR HOLDING MY HEART WHEN I DIDN'T KNOW HOW TO ASK, AND FOR SHOWING ME THAT YOUR GOODNESS IS NOT EARNED — IT'S GIVEN. THANK YOU FOR WALKING WITH ME THROUGH EVERY "WHAT IF," AND FOR TURNING MY FEARS INTO FAITH. MAY THIS STORY REFLECT YOUR GRACE, AND MAY EVERY READER FEEL THE WARMTH OF YOUR LOVE IN THEIR OWN JOURNEY. AMEN.

WHAT IF MY STORY COULD LIGHT THE WAY FOR SOMEONE ELSE?

YOU MIGHT LAUGH A LITTLE BIT ABOUT THIS WHAT IF'S OF MINE, BUT I HAVE REALLY THOUGHT ABOUT THAT WHAT IF EVERYTHING I'VE LIVED THROUGH – THE SACRIFICES, THE HEARTBREAKS, THE TRIUMPHS – WASN'T JUST FOR ME? WHAT IF MY STORY COULD LIGHT THE WAY FOR SOMEONE ELSE? I'VE COME TO BELIEVE THAT LEGACY ISN'T BUILT IN GRAND GESTURES OR PERFECT OUTCOMES. IT'S BUILT IN QUIET CHOICES, IN VALUES LIVED DAILY, AND IN THE COURAGE TO KEEP GOING WHEN NO ONE'S WATCHING. I REMEMBER WHEN I WAS IN HIGH SCHOOL, ONE OF OUR TEACHER HAVE TOLD US ABOUT THE THREE THINGS EVERY PERSON SHOULD DO TO LEAVE A LEGACY: PLANT A TREE, HAVE A CHILD AND WRITE A BOOK.

I DIDN'T SET OUT TO BUILD A LEGACY. I SET OUT TO SURVIVE. TO STUDY, TO WORK, TO LOVE, TO CREATE A LIFE THAT FELT SAFE AND MEANINGFUL. BUT SOMEWHERE ALONG THE WAY, I REALIZED THAT EVERY DECISION I MADE – EVERY BOUNDARY I SET, EVERY DOCUMENT I SUBMITTED, EVERY MOMENT I CHOSE DIGNITY OVER FEAR – WAS SHAPING SOMETHING FAR GREATER THAN JUST MY OWN FUTURE.

I THINK ABOUT MY CHILDREN, EVEN THOUGH THEY'RE FAR AWAY. I THINK ABOUT THE KIND OF STRENGTH I WANT THEM TO INHERIT – NOT JUST THE STRENGTH TO WORK HARD, BUT THE STRENGTH TO SPEAK UP, TO REST, TO LOVE WITH INTEGRITY. I WANT THEM TO KNOW THAT THEIR MOTHER DIDN'T JUST CHASE A BETTER LIFE. SHE BUILT ONE, BRICK BY BRICK, WITH GRACE AND GRIT.

I THINK ABOUT MY PARTNER, AND THE HOME WE'RE CREATING TOGETHER. A HOME THAT BLENDS CULTURES, HONORS TRUTH, AND WELCOMES LOVE IN ALL ITS FORMS. I WANT OUR STORY TO BE A REMINDER THAT HEALING IS POSSIBLE, THAT SECOND CHANCES ARE REAL, AND THAT LOVE – WHEN ROOTED IN RESPECT – CAN WEATHER ANY STORM.

I THINK ABOUT OTHER WOMEN LIKE ME. MIGRANTS. OFWS. STUDENTS. PARTNERS. MOTHERS. WOMEN WHO ARE QUIETLY CARRYING THE WEIGHT OF TWO WORLDS. I WANT THEM TO KNOW THAT THEIR STORY MATTERS. THAT THEIR VOICE IS POWERFUL. THAT THEY DON'T HAVE TO BE PERFECT TO BE WORTHY OF PEACE, JOY, AND BELONGING.

THE LEGACY I'M BUILDING IS NOT ABOUT TITLES OR WEALTH. IT'S ABOUT VALUES. HONESTY.

COMPASSION. RESILIENCE. BOUNDARIES. FAITH. IT'S ABOUT CHOOSING WHAT'S RIGHT EVEN WHEN IT'S HARD. IT'S ABOUT SHOWING UP FOR YOURSELF SO YOU CAN SHOW UP FOR OTHERS WITH AUTHENTICITY AND STRENGTH.

I HOPE MY READERS CARRY FORWARD THE MESSAGE THAT HEALING IS NOT LINEAR, AND GROWTH IS NOT LOUD. THAT SOMETIMES, THE MOST POWERFUL THING YOU CAN DO IS SAY "NO," ASK FOR HELP, OR START AGAIN. I HOPE THEY SEE THEMSELVES IN MY STORY – NOT BECAUSE IT'S PERFECT, BUT BECAUSE IT'S REAL.

IF I HAD NEVER WRITTEN THIS BOOK, MAYBE MY STORY WOULD'VE STAYED TUCKED AWAY IN QUIET CORNERS. BUT I DID WRITE IT. AND NOW, IT BELONGS TO ANYONE WHO NEEDS IT. TO ANYONE STANDING AT THE EDGE OF A DECISION, WONDERING IF THEY'RE STRONG ENOUGH. YOU ARE. AND SO WAS I.

WHAT IF MY STORY COULD LIGHT THE WAY FOR SOMEONE ELSE? I BELIEVE IT ALREADY IS. IN EVERY READER WHO FINDS COURAGE IN THESE PAGES. IN EVERY CHILD WHO SEES STRENGTH IN THEIR MOTHER'S EYES. IN EVERY WOMAN WHO CHOOSES HERSELF, EVEN WHEN THE WORLD TELLS HER NOT TO.

THIS IS THE LEGACY I'M BUILDING. NOT JUST FOR ME, BUT FOR ALL OF US WHO DARED TO ASK WHAT IF – AND FOUND SOMETHING GREATER THAN WE EVER IMAGINED.

BEYOND OF THIS BOOK

This book was never meant to end with the last sentence. It was meant to begin something—softly, bravely, and in your own time. The following pages are invitations. Not tasks nor tests. Just gentle doorways to your own "what ifs."

WHAT IF JOURNALING . . . . . .

Below are simple and heartfelt sentences you will read and these aren't just questions. They're keys. I want you to choose one each day, or let your heart pick the one it needs most.

A. WHAT IF THE VERSION OF ME I BURIED LONG AGO IS STILL WAITING TO BLOOM?

Grab a notebook or a piece of paper and let your pen speak to the dreams you paused, the talents you tucked away, the softness you thought the world couldn't hold.

B. WHAT IF I WAS NEVER BROKEN --- JUST BEAUTIFULLY REARRANGED?

Now I want you to think about one unforgettable experience that made you explore that moments that felt like endings. Did a space occur? Why did they make space for? What did they teach you about your reshaping?

C. WHAT IF I STOPPED APOLOGIZING FOR SURVIVING?

I want you to write a letter to your resilience. Name the fires you walked through and Let your strength be seen, not hidden.

D. WHAT IF MY SILENCE WAS A LANGUAGE I'M NOW READY TO TRANSLATE?

I want you to reflect on the things you didn't say. What truths are rising now? What would it feel like to speak them?

E. WHAT IF I PLANTED ONE "WHAT IF" TODAY—AND WATERED IT WITH ACTION?

Choose a small step. A whisper of courage. A gentle move toward the life you've imagined.

F. WHAT IF I AM THE ANSWER TO SOMEONE ELSE'S "WHAT IF"?

Think of the people watching you—your children, your younger self, your future readers and listeners of your life. What does your becoming unlock for them?

TIMELINE OF GRACE

This might be a little bit tricky. I wanted you to sketch your life not by achievements, but by emotional turning points. Grab a piece of paper and pen. Draw a simple line and Mark the moments that shaped you. Below is a sample that I made that you can refer to. You can add many dots for your own timeline. Have a chance to go back where you wanted to go back on that emotional turning points.

2020 — I stayed silent when I wanted to speak. I learned how to listen deeply.

2023 — I let go of a version of myself I no longer recognized. I began to breathe again.

2024 — I forgave someone who never asked. I reclaimed my peace.

2025 - 2020 — I said "yes" to a new beginning. I honored my own voice. I paused. I rested. I healed. I remembered that softness is strength.

I wrote this book. I turned my "what ifs" into a legacy.

LETTER TO A FORMER SELF

Now, its time for a a quiet conversation across time. There's a version of you who walked through fire with no map. You didn't have the words, but you kept going. This letter is not for fixing—it's for honoring. Choose a version of yourself who needed love, clarity, or courage.

Write freely—don't edit, don't explain.

Use a paper, journal, or voice notes—whatever feels safe.

You can start with:

<u>Dear Me who stayed quiet in 2013...</u>

<u>Dear Me who left everything behind in 2020...</u>

<u>Dear Me who didn't know she was worthy...</u>

You can choose a year, a season, or a moment. Then write to your former self. Speak gently. Let your former self know he/she was never alone.

CREATE YOUR OWN AFFIRMATIONS

Let your own words become anchors.
Grab a sticky note or any piece of paper. Write 5 affirmations that feel true today or everday. Use a marker so you can always see it. Feel free to decorate or be creative to them. Just like on top. Keep them close.

Remember to think this

"I am allowed to rewrite my story".
"My "what ifs" are seeds, not regrets".
"I am not too late. I am right on time".
"I am both soft and strong".
"I am becoming, even when I'm still".

QUIET COURAGE CHECKLIST

Now this is my last activity for you. Choose one small act of courage this week. Remember courage doesn't always roar. Sometimes it whispers, "Try again."

This checklist is a gentle invitation to act—not loudly, but intentionally.

I want you to pick or check one below or let one pick you. You can also write in a piece of paper, the courage checklist you wanted to do even if your not comfortable. Sounds tricky but remember, sometimes you can't fully grow if you are always in your comfort zone. Step out of it and try.

- Light a candle and sit in silence for 5 minutes
- Tell someone "thank you" for a moment they didn't know mattered
- Choose one "what if" and take a small step toward it
- Write a truth you've never spoken
- Rest without guilt
- Say "no" to something that drains you
- Say "yes" to something that scares you a little
- Revisit a chapter of your life with compassion, not critique

Let yourself be seen—just as you are

FINAL WORDS

If you've made it here, thank you. Thank you for sitting with mine and your story. For asking brave questions. For honoring the versions of you who didn't have the words—but kept going anyway.

This book was never about fixing you nor myself. It was about finding you—in the quiet, in the questions, in the grace between chapters.
You are not too late.
You are not too much.
You are not alone.
Your "what ifs" are not regrets.
They are seeds.
And you, dear reader, are the soil.
Keep blooming.
Keep becoming.

Keep walking gently toward the life that's waiting for you.

With love,

Zandra Mae

What if the choices you didn't make before shaped the life you're living today?

"Beyond the Greatest What If's" is all about the "what ifs" that come from lived experiences. This book is an invitation to reflect—not only on the author's story, but on yours. It explores the decisions that define us, the fears that challenge us, and the courage it takes to move forward, even when uncertainty whispers that we should not.

Through heartfelt reflections and honest storytelling, Zandra opens a space for readers to pause, question, and discover meaning in their own journeys. Whether you are navigating change, facing doubt, or searching for hope, this book reminds you that the "what ifs" of life can become stepping stones toward growth and resilience.

About the Author

Zandra Mae is an educator in Perth WA, Fiipina migrant, once an international student and a mother who writes with empathy and authenticity. Her work blends with personal experience with universal truths, encouraging readers to embrace both the struggles and the beauty of their paths.

www.ingramcontent.com/pod-product-compliance
Lightning Source LLC
Chambersburg PA
CBHW041216070526
44583CB00001B/11